StarKist

TUNA *for* TODAY

Tempting New Ideas

PUBLICATIONS INTERNATIONAL, LTD.

This edition published by Publications International, Ltd., 7373 N. Cicero Ave., Lincolnwood, IL 60646.

Recipe Development: Elvie Wilkenson
Photography: Sacco Productions Limited, Chicago

Pictured on the front cover: Albacore Stir-Fry *(page 74)*.

Pictured on the back cover *(top to bottom):* Tuna Fiesta Soft Taco *(page 24)*, Mini California Tuna Cakes with Remoulade Sauce *(page 12)* and Tuna and Caponata Sauce *(page 58)*.

ISBN: 0-7853-2386-4

Manufactured in U.S.A.

8 7 6 5 4 3 2 1

Prep Time: Includes the amount of time it takes to prepare and cook the recipe. The time is for such tasks as opening cans, peeling and chopping vegetables and shredding cheese, as well as baking, simmering and browning. Whenever possible, steps are combined to save time (i.e., vegetables are chopped while waiting for water to boil, etc.). However, prep time does not include the time it takes for advanced preparation of foods (i.e., steaming vegetables, cooking and cooling rice, thawing vegetables, etc.).

Microwave Cooking: Microwave ovens vary in wattage. The microwave cooking times given in this publication are approximate. Use the cooking times as guidelines and check for doneness before adding more time. Consult manufacturer's instructions for suitable microwave-safe cooking dishes.

Star Kist

TUNA for TODAY

Tempting New Ideas

TUNA *for* TODAY

People love the taste and convenience of StarKist® tuna. But besides having great flavor, tuna is a terrific food for healthy eating. Did you know that tuna is a good source of niacin and vitamin B_{12}, which are important for heart health, and the protein in tuna is easier to digest than other meat protein. Also, a two-ounce serving of StarKist Chunk Light water-packed tuna has *less cholesterol** and *less saturated fat*** than chicken or beef. These are a few of the reasons that make tuna a smart choice and a wonderful substitute for meat and poultry dishes.

When selecting tuna, choose StarKist, America's best-loved and most trusted brand.*** Our tuna products are consistently great tasting because of our strict quality controls that continually monitor the entire packing process—from the sea to the can. Our dolphin-safe policy was the first in the industry and one we are firmly committed to, along with millions of our consumers.

Charlie the Tuna
StarKist's spokefish and all-time purveyor of good taste

StarKist tuna offers meal magic to prevent menu boredom. The secret to its magic is not only its fantastic versatility, but also the ease with which delicious entrées are ready to enjoy. Many of these recipes are prepared in 30 minutes or less—a real plus for today's busy cooks. For instance, a can of tuna combined with a variety of fresh vegetables and canned tomatoes makes the sensational Tuna and Caponata Sauce. This sauce is ready to serve over your choice of pasta in an easy 25 minutes.

Those of you who like your tuna in the traditional ways—sandwiches, soups and salads—are in for a treat. There are old favorites, such as Tuna Melt, and innovative creations, such as Spicy Tuna Empanadas and Nutty Albacore Salad Pitas. These are just a sampling of the tasty tuna dishes you'll find here.

The recipes that follow suggest using Solid White (albacore) tuna or offer a choice between Solid White and Chunk Light tuna. To help guide your decision, here is some information about these different types of tuna. Solid White tuna comes from albacore tuna. It is packed as a solid fillet and is firm, white and mild. These characteristics make it a great substitute for chicken. It is often referred to as the gold standard of tuna.

Chunk Light tuna is packed in a chunk style instead of a solid fillet. It is light in color and comes from either yellowfin (ahi) or skipjack tuna. Chunk Light tuna is most commonly used in sandwiches, spreads and family-style baked dishes.

You'll enjoy the compliments from your family and friends when you serve these mouth-watering StarKist dishes. Bon Appetit!

For Chunk Light Tuna in Spring Water

*30% less cholesterol than chicken (30mg versus 43mg) and 33% less than beef (30mg versus 45mg) based on two-ounce serving

**72% less saturated fat than chicken (0.18g versus 0.65g) and 94% less than beef (0.18g versus 3.2g) based on two-ounce serving

***1992 Tuna Usage and Attitude Study

Appetizers &

◆◆◆

SNACKS

Tri-Colored Tuna Stuffed Mushrooms

This assortment of stuffed mushrooms is not just great looking; the smoked Gouda cheese complements the tuna flavor.

30 medium mushrooms, cleaned and stems removed
2 tablespoons melted butter or margarine
1 cup finely chopped onion
1 tablespoon vegetable oil
1 can (6 ounces) StarKist Solid White or Chunk Light Tuna, drained and flaked
½ cup shredded smoked Gouda cheese, divided
1 red bell pepper, seeded and puréed*
1 package (10 ounces) frozen spinach soufflé
¼ cup mayonnaise, divided
¼ cup grated Parmesan cheese, divided
½ teaspoon curry powder

Lightly coat mushroom caps with melted butter; divide into 3 groups of 10. Sauté onions in hot oil until tender. *In each of 3 small bowls,* place ⅓ tuna and ⅓ sautéed onions. In first small bowl, add ¼ cup Gouda cheese and red bell pepper purée.

In second small bowl, add ¼ cup spinach soufflé,** 2 tablespoons mayonnaise, 2 tablespoons Parmesan cheese and curry powder. In third small bowl, add remaining ¼ cup Gouda cheese, remaining 2 tablespoons mayonnaise and remaining 2 tablespoons Parmesan cheese. Fill 10 mushrooms with filling from each bowl. Arrange on baking sheet; bake in 350°F oven 10 to 12 minutes. Serve hot.

Makes 30 servings

*To purée bell pepper: Place seeded and coarsely chopped red pepper into blender or food processor with metal blade. Blend or process until puréed.

**Keep remainder frozen until ready to use.

Prep Time: 40 minutes

Tri-Colored Tuna Stuffed Mushrooms

Tuna and Olive Spread

This quick and easy spread will be a family favorite in no time.

> **1 can (6 ounces) StarKist Solid White or Chunk Light Tuna, drained**
> **1 hard-cooked egg *or* 2 hard-cooked egg whites**
> **½ cup soft cream cheese**
> **¼ cup prepared green onion dip**
> **1 can (4¼ ounces) chopped ripe olives**
> **Salt and pepper to taste**
> **Snipped chives and paprika, for garnish**
> **Crackers, assorted breads or raw vegetables**

In food processor bowl with metal blade, place tuna, egg, cream cheese and onion dip; process until smooth. Transfer to bowl; stir in olives, salt and pepper. Chill several hours or overnight before serving. Serve or mold into special shape, if desired. Garnish with chives and paprika. Serve with crackers.

Makes about 12 servings

Prep Time: 5 minutes

Creamy Tuna Dip with Dill

Whip up this dip using lighter ingredients for great taste with less guilt.

> **1 can (6 ounces) StarKist Solid White or Chunk Light Tuna, drained and chunked**
> **1 package (8 ounces) light cream cheese**
> **½ cup light mayonnaise**
> **½ cup light sour cream**
> **2 green onions, including tops, cut into 1-inch pieces**
> **1 tablespoon dried dill weed**
> **2 teaspoons lemon juice**
> **½ teaspoon garlic salt**
> **¼ teaspoon white pepper**
> **Fresh raw vegetables for dipping**

In food processor bowl with metal blade, place tuna, cream cheese, mayonnaise, sour cream, onions, dill, lemon juice, garlic salt and white pepper. Pulse on and off until blended. Pour into small bowl; chill several hours or overnight before serving with vegetables.

Makes 8 to 10 servings

Note: Mixture will be soft. For firmer dip, use regular cream cheese, mayonnaise and sour cream in place of the light varieties.

Prep Time: 5 minutes

Tuna and Olive Spread

Mini California Tuna Cakes with Remoulade Sauce

These delectable little bites will not last long.

- 3 tablespoons butter or margarine
- ½ cup minced celery
- ¼ cup minced green onions, including tops
- ¼ cup minced red bell pepper
- 3 large eggs, beaten
- 1 tablespoon Dijon-style mustard
- ½ cup half & half or whipping cream
- 3½ to 4 cups fresh breadcrumbs, divided
- 2 tablespoons minced fresh parsley
- 1 can (12 ounces) StarKist Solid White or Chunk Light Tuna, drained and finely flaked
- Salt and pepper to taste
- Olive oil and butter, as needed
- Remoulade Sauce (recipe follows)

In small saucepan, melt 3 tablespoons butter over medium heat. Add celery, onions and red pepper; sauté until onions are soft. Cool. In large bowl, combine eggs, mustard, half & half and sautéed vegetables; mix well. Stir in about 3½ cups breadcrumbs, parsley and tuna; add salt and pepper. Chill at least 3 hours. Shape into small balls, using about 2 tablespoons mixture; flatten slightly. (If tuna mixture is too moist to shape, add more breadcrumbs.) In large skillet, heat several tablespoons olive oil and butter over medium-high heat until hot; sauté mini tuna cakes in batches about 1 minute per side. Remove from skillet; keep warm in 300°F oven. Serve immediately with Remoulade Sauce.

Makes 20 servings

Note: If you prefer a crisper exterior, lightly coat each tuna cake with dry breadcrumbs before sautéing.

Tip: For dinner-sized tuna cakes, shape into patties 2½ inches wide and ¾ inch thick; sauté about 4 minutes per side.

Prep Time: 20 minutes

Remoulade Sauce

- 1 cup mayonnaise
- 2 tablespoons whole grain Dijon-style mustard
- 2 tablespoons finely chopped gherkins
- 2 tablespoons drained chopped capers
- 1 tablespoon minced fresh parsley
- 1 teaspoon dried tarragon, crushed
- ½ teaspoon freshly grated lemon peel
- ½ teaspoon ground black pepper
- Salt to taste

In blender or food processor bowl with metal blade, combine all ingredients; blend well. Chill several hours before serving with Mini California Tuna Cakes.

Prep Time: 5 minutes

Mini California Tuna Cakes with Remoulade Sauce

Hot Artichoke and Tuna Spread

This hot appetizer spread is excellent on plain or toasted French bread and assorted crackers. It's a great addition to any cocktail party.

- **1 can (6 ounces) StarKist Solid White or Chunk Light Tuna, drained**
- **1 jar (12 ounces) marinated artichoke hearts, drained**
- **1 to 2 cloves garlic**
- **1 cup shredded mozzarella cheese**
- **½ cup grated Parmesan cheese**
- **¼ cup chopped canned green chiles**
- **1 tablespoon minced green onion**
- **2 to 3 tablespoons mayonnaise Hot pepper sauce to taste French bread or assorted crackers**

In food processor bowl with metal blade, place all ingredients except bread. Process until well blended but not puréed. Transfer mixture to ovenproof serving dish. Bake, uncovered, in 350°F oven about 30 minutes or until mixture is golden. Serve hot with French bread.

Makes 12 servings

Note: This mixture may be baked in small hollowed bread shell. Wrap in foil; bake as above. Open top of foil last 5 minutes of baking.

Tip: Mixture keeps well, tightly covered, in refrigerator for up to 5 days.

Prep Time: 35 minutes

Tuna Potato Boats

This hearty appetizer can double as a light meal.

- **4 russet potatoes, baked and halved lengthwise**
- **1 can (12 ounces) StarKist Solid White or Chunk Light Tuna, drained and flaked**
- **¾ cup shredded Cheddar cheese**
- **¼ cup finely chopped green onions**
- **¼ cup cooked and crumbled bacon**
- **¼ cup sour cream**

Scoop out potatoes, leaving ¼-inch shells; place potato pulp in bowl. Add tuna, cheese, onions, bacon and sour cream; mix just enough to blend together but still remain chunky. Spoon into potato shells. Bake in 375°F oven 15 minutes or until potatoes are hot and cheese is melted. *Makes 8 servings*

Tip: Use microwave to cook potatoes and heat finished stuffed potatoes.

Prep Time: 30 minutes

Hot Artichoke and Tuna Spread

Tuna in Crispy Won Ton Cups

This is great for kids to make.

**18 won ton skins, *each*
3¼ inches square
Butter or olive oil cooking
spray
1 can (6 ounces) StarKist Solid
White or Chunk Light Tuna,
drained and flaked
⅓ cup cold cooked orzo (rice-
shaped pasta) or cooked rice
¼ cup Southwestern ranch-style
vegetable dip with jalapeños
or other sour cream dip
¼ cup drained pimiento-stuffed
green olives, chopped
3 tablespoons sweet pickle
relish, drained
Paprika, for garnish
Parsley sprigs, for garnish**

Cut won tons into circles with 3-inch round cookie cutter. Spray miniature muffin pans with cooking spray. Place one circle in each muffin cup; press to sides to mold won ton to cup. Spray each won ton with cooking spray. Bake in 350°F oven 6 to 8 minutes or until golden brown; set aside.

In small bowl, gently mix tuna, orzo, dip, olives and relish. Refrigerate filling until ready to serve. Remove won ton cups from muffin pan. Use rounded teaspoon to fill each cup; garnish with paprika and parsley.

Makes 18 servings

Tip: Cups may be made a day ahead; store in airtight container. Reheat in 350°F oven 1 to 2 minutes to recrisp.

Prep Time: 20 minutes

Tuna Tapenade

Tapenade is a flavorful spread made in the South of France. Serve with brightly colored fresh vegetables, or use to stuff tomatoes or hard-cooked eggs.

**1 can (12 ounces) StarKist Solid
White or Chunk Light Tuna,
drained and chunked
1 can (6 ounces) pitted ripe
olives, drained
4 to 6 anchovy fillets, drained
¼ cup drained capers
2 tablespoons lemon juice
1 tablespoon Dijon-style
mustard
1 teaspoon dried basil
⅛ teaspoon ground black pepper
2 cloves garlic
⅓ cup extra-virgin olive oil
Raw vegetables, crisp wheat
crackers or pita bread**

In food processor bowl with metal blade, place tuna, olives, anchovies, capers, lemon juice, mustard, basil, pepper and garlic. Add oil very slowly through feed tube while processing. Chill several hours before serving with vegetables.

Makes 12 servings

Prep Time: 7 minutes

Tuna in Crispy Won Ton Cups

Tuna Mushroom Pâté with Orange Liqueur

Guests will devour this zesty, orange-flavored spread. It is easy to prepare in a food processor.

  2 cloves garlic
  ½ medium white onion
  2 tablespoons butter
  1 jar (4½ ounces) sliced
     mushrooms, drained
  2 tablespoons orange liqueur or
     orange juice
  1 package (8 ounces) cream
     cheese, softened
  1 can (12 ounces) StarKist Solid
     White or Chunk Light Tuna,
     drained
  2 tablespoons fresh parsley
     leaves
  1 teaspoon grated orange peel
  ¼ teaspoon salt
  ¼ teaspoon coarsely ground
     black pepper
  ½ cup toasted slivered almonds
     (optional)
     Crackers or raw vegetables

In food processor bowl with metal blade, drop garlic through feed tube while processing. Add onion; pulse on and off to chop coarsely. In small skillet, melt butter over medium heat. Add garlic and onion; sauté until onion is soft. Add mushrooms and liqueur; cook until liquid evaporates. Cool.

In same food processor bowl with metal blade, place cream cheese, tuna, parsley, orange peel, salt and pepper. Pulse on and off to blend. Add cooled onion-mushroom mixture; pulse on and off to blend. Stir in almonds, if desired. Spoon into 1-quart serving bowl; chill several hours or overnight. Serve with crackers.

Makes about 12 servings

Prep Time: 20 minutes

Tuna 'n' Celery Sticks

This is a great snack for kids! Let everyone fill their own celery sticks with prepared filling.

  4 ounces cream cheese, softened
  3 tablespoons plain yogurt or
     mayonnaise
  1½ teaspoons dried basil
  1 can (12 ounces) StarKist Solid
     White or Chunk Light Tuna,
     drained and flaked
  ½ cup finely grated carrot or
     zucchini
  ½ cup finely shredded Cheddar
     cheese
  2 teaspoons instant minced
     onion
  10 to 12 celery stalks, cleaned,
     strings removed

In large bowl, mix together cream cheese, yogurt and basil until smooth. Add tuna, carrot, Cheddar cheese and onion; mix well. Spread mixture into celery stalks; cut into fourths.   *Makes 40 servings*

Prep Time: 10 minutes

*Tuna Mushroom Pâté with
Orange Liqueur*

Soups &

SANDWICHES

Albacore Corn Chowder

This chowder is a thick, rich soup with chunks of tuna and vegetables.

2 tablespoons butter or
   margarine
½ cup sliced celery
½ cup chopped onion
¾ cup chopped carrot
2 to 3 tablespoons flour
1 teaspoon dried thyme or
   Italian seasoning
1 can (17 ounces) cream-style
   corn
2 cups milk
1 can (12 ounces) StarKist Solid
   White Tuna, drained and
   flaked
1 cup water
1 teaspoon chicken flavor
   instant bouillon

In medium saucepan, melt butter over medium heat; sauté celery, onion and carrot about 3 minutes. Add flour and thyme; blend well. Cook 3 more minutes. Add corn, milk, tuna, water and bouillon, stirring to blend. Cover and simmer *(do not boil)* 5 minutes to heat through, stirring occasionally.

Makes 4 servings

Prep Time: 20 minutes

Peanut-ty Tuna Sandwiches

This recipe combines interesting flavors and textures.

3 tablespoons mayonnaise
2 tablespoons crunchy-style
   peanut butter
¼ teaspoon curry powder
¼ teaspoon lemon peel
1 can (6 ounces) StarKist Solid
   White or Chunk Light Tuna,
   drained and flaked
1 tablespoon finely minced
   green onion
8 slices whole wheat bread
4 lettuce leaves (optional)
4 tomato slices (optional)

In small bowl, combine mayonnaise, peanut butter, curry powder and lemon peel; blend well. In medium bowl, combine tuna and onion; stir in mayonnaise mixture. Spread onto 4 slices of bread. Add lettuce leaves and tomato slices, if desired; top with remaining 4 bread slices.

Makes 4 servings

Prep Time: 8 minutes

Albacore Corn Chowder

Tuna Melt

A great tasting sandwich, anytime.

> 1 can (12 ounces) StarKist Solid White or Chunk Light Tuna, drained and flaked
> 1/3 cup mayonnaise
> 1½ tablespoons sweet pickle relish
> 1½ tablespoons chopped onion
> ½ tablespoon mustard
> 3 English muffins, split and toasted
> 6 tomato slices, halved
> 6 slices American, Cheddar, Swiss or Monterey Jack cheese
> Fresh fruit (optional)

In medium bowl, combine tuna, mayonnaise, pickle relish, onion and mustard; mix well. Spread about 1/3 cup on each muffin half. Top with tomato slice and cheese slice. Broil 4 to 5 minutes or until cheese melts. Serve with fresh fruit, if desired.

Makes 6 servings

Note: For a festive look, cut each slice of cheese into strips. Arrange in a decorative pattern over sandwiches.

Prep Time: 15 minutes

Tuna Pizza with Caponata and Prosciutto

Italian caponata is a relish of eggplant, tomatoes, olives, onions and capers.

> 1 package (1 pound) Italian bread shell for pizza
> 2 teaspoons olive oil
> 1 can (7½ ounces) caponata
> 1 can (6 ounces) StarKist Solid White Tuna, drained and chunked
> 8 slices (1 ounce) prosciutto
> 2 to 3 plum tomatoes, sliced ¼ inch thick
> 1 cup crumbled feta cheese
> 1 cup shredded mozzarella cheese
> Crushed red pepper (optional)

Place bread shell on foil-lined baking sheet; brush to edge with oil. Spread caponata to within 1 inch of edge. Top with tuna, prosciutto, tomatoes, feta and mozzarella cheeses. Bake in 450°F oven 10 to 12 minutes or until cheeses are melted and pizza is heated through. Cool 1 minute before slicing. Serve with crushed red pepper, if desired.

Makes 4 servings

Prep Time: 20 minutes

Tuna Melt

Tuna Fiesta Soft Tacos

For a change of pace use tortillas for wrapping other sandwich fillings.

⅓ cup mayonnaise
½ teaspoon garlic salt
½ teaspoon lemon pepper
    seasoning
1 can (6 ounces) StarKist Solid
    White or Chunk Light Tuna,
    drained and flaked
¼ cup chopped celery
1 hard-cooked egg, chopped
2 tablespoons finely chopped
    green onion, including tops
2 tablespoons finely chopped
    green bell pepper
1 tablespoon drained chopped
    pimiento
6 flour tortillas (6 inches *each*),
    warmed
1 cup shredded iceberg lettuce
½ cup shredded Colby or
    Monterey Jack cheese
    Salsa (optional)

In large bowl, combine mayonnaise, garlic salt, lemon pepper seasoning, tuna, celery, egg, onion, bell pepper and pimiento; mix thoroughly. Place generous ¼ cup filling on one side of each tortilla; top with lettuce and cheese. Fold tortilla over; serve with salsa, if desired.

Makes 6 servings

Prep Time: 10 minutes

Potato and Albacore Chowder

If you love seafood chowders, you will love the smooth, rich flavor and easy preparation of this recipe.

2 tablespoons butter or
    margarine
¼ cup chopped onion
¼ cup chopped celery
1 cup chopped or grated cooked
    potatoes
1 can (10¾ ounces) cream of
    potato soup
⅔ cup milk or half & half
⅔ cup chicken broth
1 can (6 ounces) StarKist Solid
    White Tuna, drained and
    chunked
    Freshly ground black pepper
    Shredded Cheddar cheese
    Snipped chives

In medium saucepan, melt butter over medium heat. Sauté onion and celery until onion is tender. Add potatoes; continue cooking 2 to 3 minutes. Add soup, milk, chicken broth and tuna; heat thoroughly over low heat. Top each serving with pepper, cheese and chives.

Makes 2 servings

Tip: Recipe is easily doubled.

Prep Time: 10 minutes

Tuna Fiesta Soft Taco

StarKist Vegetable Gazpacho

Broiled or grilled vegetables lend a hearty, roasted flavor to this adaptation of a classic soup.

    1 large onion, quartered
    1 medium zucchini, halved
        lengthwise
    1 yellow or crookneck squash,
        halved lengthwise
    1 red bell pepper
    1 yellow bell pepper
 ³⁄₄ cup bottled olive oil vinaigrette
        dressing
    1 can (6 ounces) StarKist Solid
        White Tuna, drained and
        chunked
    3 pounds firm ripe tomatoes,
        chopped
    2 cucumbers, peeled, seeded and
        chopped
    2 to 3 cloves fresh garlic,
        minced or pressed
 ½ cup fresh sourdough
        breadcrumbs
 1½ to 2 cups tomato juice

Preheat broiler. Brush onion quarters, zucchini and squash halves and whole peppers with dressing; reserve remaining dressing. Broil 6 to 8 minutes, turning occasionally until vegetables are roasted and pepper skins blister and turn black. Remove from broiler. Place peppers in paper bag; close bag and let stand 15 minutes before peeling. Cool remaining vegetables. Peel skin from peppers; seed and remove membrane. Cut all roasted vegetables in large pieces; place in food processor bowl with metal blade. Process until coarsely chopped. Transfer to large bowl; add tuna, tomatoes, cucumbers, garlic, breadcrumbs, 1½ cups tomato juice and remaining dressing. Blend thoroughly. Add remaining ½ cup tomato juice to thin, if necessary.

Makes 6 to 8 servings

Prep Time: 30 minutes

Tuna Supper Sandwiches

Kids love making and eating these super supper buns.

    2 cups shredded Cheddar cheese
 ⅓ cup chopped green onions,
        including tops
 ⅓ cup chopped red bell pepper
    1 can (2¼ ounces) sliced ripe
        olives, drained
    2 tablespoons minced fresh
        parsley
    1 teaspoon curry powder
        Seasoned salt to taste
    1 can (12 ounces) StarKist Solid
        White or Chunk Light Tuna,
        drained and chunked
 ½ cup light mayonnaise
    6 soft French rolls (7 inches
        each), halved lengthwise

In medium bowl, place cheese, onions, red pepper, olives, parsley, curry powder and salt; mix lightly. Add tuna and mayonnaise; toss lightly with fork. Cover baking sheet with foil; place rolls on foil. Spread about ⅓ cup mixture on each half. Bake in 450°F oven 10 to 12 minutes or until tops are bubbling and beginning to brown. Cool slightly before serving.

Makes 12 servings

Prep Time: 18 minutes

StarKist Vegetable Gazpacho

Spicy Tuna Empanadas

Kids will enjoy making and eating these empanadas.

> 1 can (6 ounces) StarKist Solid White or Chunk Light Tuna, drained and flaked
> 1 can (4 ounces) diced green chiles, drained
> 1 can (2¼ ounces) sliced ripe olives, drained
> ½ cup shredded sharp Cheddar cheese
> 1 chopped hard-cooked egg
> Salt and pepper to taste
> ¼ teaspoon hot pepper sauce
> ¼ cup medium thick and chunky salsa
> 2 packages (15 ounces *each*) refrigerated pie crusts
> Additional salsa

In medium bowl, place tuna, chiles, olives, cheese, egg, salt, pepper and hot pepper sauce; toss lightly with fork. Add ¼ cup salsa and toss again; set aside. Following directions on package, unfold crusts (roll out slightly with rolling pin if you prefer thinner crust); cut 4 circles, 4 inches *each*, out of each crust. Place 8 circles on foil-covered baking sheets; wet edge of each circle with water. Top each circle with ¼ cup lightly packed tuna mixture. Top with remaining circles, stretching pastry slightly to fit; press edges together and crimp with fork. Cut slits in top crust to vent. Bake in 425°F oven 15 to 18 minutes or until golden brown. Cool slightly. Serve with additional salsa.   *Makes 8 empanadas*

Prep Time: 25 minutes

Tuna and Watercress Tea Sandwiches

Tea sandwiches were never this easy; the food processor makes quick work of blending the ingredients. Now, just boil the water for tea.

> 1 can (6 ounces) StarKist Solid White Tuna, drained and chunked
> ½ cup butter or margarine, softened
> ½ cup watercress leaves, firmly packed
> 2 tablespoons lemon juice
> ¼ teaspoon salt
> ⅛ teaspoon white pepper
> 24 slices thin white or wheat sandwich bread, crusts removed
> Additional watercress, for garnish

In food processor bowl with metal blade, place tuna, butter, ½ cup watercress, lemon juice, salt and white pepper. Pulse on and off until watercress is finely chopped and mixture is blended. Spread tuna mixture on half the bread slices; top with remaining slices. Cut into squares or triangles. Serve or refrigerate up to 2 hours. Garnish with additional watercress.
          Makes 12 servings

Note: Day-old bread is best for making tea sandwiches; it is easier to slice. Use a serrated knife.

Prep Time: 15 minutes

Spicy Tuna Empanadas

New York Deli-Style Tuna

For an authentic taste, use real New York style bagels that have a shiny crust and firm texture.

- 1 can (6 ounces) StarKist Solid White Tuna, drained and flaked
- 1 hard-cooked egg, minced
- 3 tablespoons minced celery
- 1 tablespoon chopped ripe olives
- 3 to 4 tablespoons mayonnaise
- 2 teaspoons mustard (optional)
- 1 tablespoon drained capers (optional)
- 3 New York style bagels, split
- 3 ounces cream cheese, softened
  Baby kosher dill pickles, thinly sliced lengthwise
  Thinly sliced red onion rings

In medium bowl, combine tuna, egg, celery, olives and mayonnaise. Stir in mustard and capers, if desired; blend well. Chill.

To serve, toast bagels; spread each half with ½ ounce cream cheese. Top *each* with 3 pickle slices, about 3 tablespoons tuna mixture and red onion rings; serve open face.

Makes 6 servings

Prep Time: 10 minutes

Herbed Albacore Toasts

This is an interesting version of a hot sandwich with Italian herbs and Parmesan cheese lending a special flavor to the tuna.

- 1 can (6 ounces) StarKist Solid White Tuna, drained and flaked
- 3 tablespoons mayonnaise
- 2 tablespoons finely chopped onion
- ¼ to ½ teaspoon dried basil, crushed
- ¼ teaspoon dried oregano, crushed
- 4 slices (¾ inch *each*) Italian or French bread
- 2 tablespoons grated Parmesan cheese

In medium bowl, combine tuna, mayonnaise, onion and herbs; mix well. Spread ¼ tuna mixture on each slice of bread. Sprinkle with cheese; broil until cheese is golden and bubbly.   *Makes 2 servings*

Prep Time: 5 minutes

New York Deli-Style Tuna

Tuna Minestrone with Parmesan Cheese

An almost instant soup prepared from items in your pantry and freezer.

2 cans (14 1/2 ounces *each*) chicken broth *plus* water to equal 4 cups
1 can (14 1/2 ounces) ready-cut Italian-style tomatoes, undrained
1 can (15 1/4 ounces) kidney beans, drained
1/4 cup tomato paste
1 teaspoon Italian herb seasoning
1/2 teaspoon salt
1/8 teaspoon ground red pepper
1/2 cup uncooked small shell pasta
2 cups Italian-style frozen vegetables (zucchini, carrots, cauliflower, Italian green beans, lima beans)
1 can (12 ounces) StarKist Solid White Tuna, drained and chunked
3 cups fresh romaine lettuce, cut crosswise in 1-inch strips
   Freshly grated Parmesan cheese

In 4-quart saucepan, combine chicken broth mixture, tomatoes with liquid, kidney beans, tomato paste, herb seasoning, salt and red pepper; bring to a boil over high heat. Add pasta and frozen vegetables; simmer 8 minutes. Remove from heat; add tuna and romaine. Serve with cheese.

Makes 6 to 8 servings

Prep Time: 10 minutes

Tuna Torpedoes

When you have a crowd clamoring for a tuna sandwich, here's one way to feed them fast.

1 loaf (1 pound) French or Italian bread, halved lengthwise
1/4 to 1/3 cup mayonnaise
1/2 teaspoon Italian herb seasoning
   Lettuce leaves
8 tomato slices
1 can (12 ounces) StarKist Solid White or Chunk Light Tuna, drained and flaked
2 tablespoons minced onion
1 cup shredded mozzarella cheese

In hot oven or broiler, toast bread; spread both halves with mayonnaise. Sprinkle with herb seasoning. On bottom halves arrange lettuce leaves and tomato slices. Top with tuna, onion and cheese. In hot oven or broiler, heat until cheese melts. Place halves together to make a torpedo; cut into serving pieces.

Makes 4 to 6 servings

Prep Time: 15 minutes

Tuna Minestrone with Parmesan Cheese

Mini Tuna Tarts

This is an easy recipe for kids to make and it's also great for a picnic.

> 1 can (6 ounces) StarKist Solid White or Chunk Light Tuna, drained and flaked
> 2 tablespoons mayonnaise
> 2 tablespoons sweet pickle relish
> 1 green onion, including tops, minced
> ¾ cup shredded Monterey Jack cheese
> Salt and pepper to taste
> 1 package (10 count) refrigerated flaky biscuits

In small bowl, combine tuna, mayonnaise, pickle relish, onion and cheese; mix well. Add salt and pepper. Separate each biscuit into 2 halves. Press each half in bottom of lightly greased muffin pan to form a cup. Spoon scant tablespoon tuna mixture into each muffin cup. Bake in 400°F oven 8 to 10 minutes or until edges of biscuits are just golden. Serve hot or cold.

Makes 20 servings

Prep Time: 15 minutes

Chunky Albacore Chowder

A savory, piping hot chowder that will satisfy the hunger of everyone in your family.

> 1 can (10¾ ounces) low fat cream of broccoli soup
> 1 can (10¾ ounces) low fat cream of mushroom soup
> 1¼ cups low fat milk, divided
> 1 teaspoon ground cumin
> 4 to 6 drops hot pepper sauce
> ⅓ cup red bell pepper, chopped in ¼-inch pieces
> ⅓ cup chopped green onions, including tops
> ½ cup light sour cream
> 1 can (6 ounces) StarKist Solid White Tuna, drained and chunked
> ⅓ cup fresh cilantro or parsley leaves, lightly packed, finely minced
> ½ teaspoon salt
> ¼ teaspoon white pepper

In 2-quart saucepan, mix together soups, milk, cumin and hot pepper sauce. Heat over medium heat about 5 minutes, stirring occasionally. Add red pepper and onions; whisk in sour cream. Stir in tuna; heat gently (*do not boil*). Stir cilantro, salt and white pepper into soup.

Makes 4 servings

Prep Time: 15 minutes

Mini Tuna Tarts

Nutty Albacore Salad Pitas

What a great combination of tastes and textures!

    1 can (6 ounces) StarKist Solid
        White Tuna, drained and
        flaked
 ½ cup mayonnaise
 ⅓ cup chopped celery
 ¼ cup raisins or seedless grape
        halves
 ¼ cup chopped walnuts, pecans
        or almonds
 ½ teaspoon dried dill weed
        Salt and pepper to taste
    2 pita breads, halved
        Curly leaf lettuce leaves

In medium bowl, combine tuna, mayonnaise, celery, raisins, nuts and dill; mix well. Add salt and pepper. Line each pita bread pocket with lettuce leaf; fill with ¼ tuna mixture.
Makes 4 servings

Prep Time: 10 minutes

Tuna Bruschetta

This delicious light sandwich combines tomatoes, tuna, mozzarella cheese and lots of garlic in a flavor packed topping for bread.

    4 cloves garlic
 ¼ cup extra-virgin olive oil
    8 slices (½ to ¾ inch thick
        each) toasted French bread,
        about 3½×5½ inches
    2 cups chopped plum tomatoes
    1 cup shredded mozzarella
        cheese or chopped fresh
        mozzarella, drained
    1 can (6 ounces) StarKist Solid
        White or Chunk Light Tuna,
        drained and flaked
    2 tablespoons minced fresh
        parsley
 ½ teaspoon salt (optional)
        Coarsely ground black pepper
        Bibb lettuce

In blender or food processor bowl with metal blade, blend garlic and oil. Brush oil mixture on one side of each piece of toast; reserve remaining oil mixture. In medium bowl, lightly combine tomatoes, oil mixture. Add salt, if desired and pepper. Mound about ½ cup tuna mixture over each piece of toast. Place 2 pieces of toast on each lettuce-lined salad plate.
Makes 4 servings

Prep Time: 20 minutes

Nutty Albacore Salad Pita

Fabulous

◆◆◆

SALADS

Thai-Style Tuna and Fruit Salad with Sweet-Sour-Spicy Dressing

This dressing skimps on fat, but has a rich taste.

8 lettuce leaves (use different varieties for color)
2 tablespoons chopped fresh cilantro
2 tablespoons chopped fresh mint leaves
1 can (6 ounces) StarKist Solid White Tuna, drained and chunked
⅓ cup sliced cucumber
⅓ cup drained mandarin oranges
⅓ cup red seedless grape halves
¼ cup thinly sliced red onion
Sweet-Sour-Spicy Dressing (recipe follows)
⅓ cup chopped cashews or peanuts

On platter, arrange half of lettuce. Break up remaining lettuce into bite-sized pieces and place over lettuce on platter. Sprinkle cilantro and mint over lettuce. Arrange tuna, cucumber, oranges, grapes and onion on top. Refrigerate, covered, while preparing Sweet-Sour-Spicy Dressing. Pour dressing over salad; sprinkle with cashews.

Makes 4 servings

Variation: Chop or tear all lettuce into bite-sized pieces; combine with remaining ingredients. Toss with dressing.

Sweet-Sour-Spicy Dressing

Lime
3 cloves garlic
2 serrano chiles, halved, seeded and cut in pieces
¼ cup lime juice
1½ tablespoons nam pla (fish sauce) or soy sauce
1 tablespoon sugar

Peel ½ of lime with vegetable peeler. In blender or small food processor, place lime peel, garlic, chiles, lime juice, nam pla and sugar. Process until mixture is blended and lime peel, garlic and chiles are finely chopped.

Prep Time: 20 minutes

Thai-Style Tuna and Fruit Salad with Sweet-Sour-Spicy Dressing

Albacore Salad Puttanesca with Garlic Vinaigrette

This dish may become a staple in your meal planning.

- **2 cups cooked, chilled angel hair pasta**
- **2 cups chopped, peeled plum tomatoes**
- **1 can (4¼ ounces) chopped* ripe olives, drained**
- **1 cup Garlic Vinaigrette Dressing (recipe follows)**
- **1 can (6 ounces) StarKist Solid White Tuna, drained and flaked**
- **¼ cup chopped fresh basil leaves**

In large bowl, combine chilled pasta, tomatoes, olives and 1 cup Garlic Vinaigrette Dressing. Add tuna and basil leaves; toss. Serve immediately.
Makes 2 servings

*If you prefer, the olives may be sliced rather than chopped.

Garlic Vinaigrette Dressing

- **⅓ cup red wine vinegar**
- **2 tablespoons lemon juice**
- **1 to 2 cloves garlic, minced or pressed**
- **1 teaspoon freshly ground black pepper**
- **Salt to taste**
- **1 cup olive oil**

In small bowl, whisk together vinegar, lemon juice, garlic, pepper and salt. Slowly add oil, whisking continuously, until well blended.

Prep Time: 10 minutes

StarKist Salad Niçoise

Enjoy this classic tuna salad.

- **¾ pound new red potatoes, cooked in their jackets, chilled and diced**
- **1½ pounds fresh green beans, trimmed and blanched**
- **8 sliced plum tomatoes *or* 1 pint cherry tomatoes, halved**
- **¾ cup niçoise olives or halved ripe olives**
- **½ cup thinly sliced red onion rings**
- **3 tablespoons finely chopped Italian parsley**
- **¾ teaspoon medium-grind black pepper**
- **Salt to taste**
- **4 hard-cooked eggs, cut in quarters**
- **1 can (12 ounces) StarKist Solid White Tuna, drained and chunked**
- **1 cup bottled vinaigrette dressing, divided**

On large platter, arrange all ingredients except dressing. Cover with plastic wrap; chill. Just before serving, drizzle about ½ cup dressing over all ingredients; serve remaining dressing on side.
Makes 4 to 6 servings

Note: Look for niçoise olives in gourmet section of supermarket or in Italian deli.

Prep Time: 30 minutes

Albacore Salad Puttanesca with Garlic Vinaigrette

Albacore and White Bean Salad with Orange Dressing

Feature this quick and easy salad at your next barbecue.

- 2 cans (15 ounces *each*) Great Northern beans, rinsed and drained
- 3 hard-cooked eggs, chopped
- 1/3 cup chopped green onions, including tops
- 1/3 cup chopped red onion
- 3/4 teaspoon salt
- 1/3 cup bottled Italian dressing
- 1 tablespoon frozen orange juice concentrate, thawed
- 2 teaspoons grated orange peel
- 1/2 to 1 teaspoon crushed red pepper
- 1 can (6 ounces) StarKist Solid White Tuna, drained and chunked
- 2 chopped plum tomatoes, drained
  Quartered orange slices, for garnish

In large bowl, combine beans, eggs, onions and salt. In glass measuring cup, blend dressing, orange juice concentrate, peel and crushed red pepper. Add to salad in bowl. Chill several hours or overnight. Just before serving, gently toss in tuna and tomatoes. Garnish with orange slices.   *Makes 6 servings*

Prep Time: 15 minutes

Albacore Waldorf Salad

The original Waldorf Salad was created in the 1890's, and has gone through many changes and adaptations. We know you'll like this one.

- 3 medium apples, cored and cubed
- 2 tablespoons lemon juice
- 1 cup chopped celery
- 1/3 cup raisins
- 1/3 cup chopped walnuts or pecans
- 1 can (12 ounces) StarKist Solid White Tuna, drained and chunked
- 1/2 cup mayonnaise
- 1/4 cup milk
- 1/4 teaspoon ground cinnamon
  Sugar to taste (optional)

In large bowl, toss together apples and lemon juice. Add celery, raisins, walnuts and tuna; toss gently. In medium bowl, combine mayonnaise, milk and cinnamon; blend well. For a sweeter dressing, add sugar. Pour dressing over apple-tuna mixture; toss gently to coat.
          Makes 6 servings

Prep Time: 10 minutes

Albacore and White Bean Salad with Orange Dressing

Marinated Albacore and Mushroom Salad with Quick Sour Cream Dressing

A cool refreshing salad in no time.

- 1 can (6 ounces) StarKist Solid White Tuna, drained and chunked
- 1 pound mushrooms, cleaned and quartered
- 1/4 cup chopped green onions, including tops
- 2 tablespoons minced fresh parsley
- 2 tablespoons lemon juice
- 2 teaspoons sugar
- 1/4 teaspoon salt
- 1/4 teaspoon white pepper
  Quick Sour Cream Dressing (recipe follows)
  Bibb lettuce
- 3 or 4 tomatoes, sliced or wedged, for garnish

In medium bowl, combine tuna, mushrooms, onions, parsley, lemon juice, sugar, salt and white pepper. Refrigerate, covered, 1 to 3 hours or until ready to serve. Just before serving, prepare Quick Sour Cream Dressing; fold into tuna mixture. Serve on lettuce-lined plates. Garnish with tomatoes.

Makes 6 servings

Quick Sour Cream Dressing
- 1/2 cup whipping cream
- 1/2 teaspoon salt
- 1/2 teaspoon dry mustard
- 1/4 cup sour cream

In small bowl, beat whipping cream with salt and dry mustard until thickened; fold in sour cream.

Prep Time: 15 minutes

Albacore and Spinach Salad

Choose spinach leaves that are crisp and dark green.

- 1 bunch fresh spinach, washed, stemmed and torn
- 1/2 pound mushrooms, cleaned and sliced
- 1/2 medium red onion, thinly sliced
- 1 avocado, peeled and cut in 1/2-inch cubes
- 1 can (12 ounces) StarKist Solid White Tuna, drained and chunked
- 1/2 cup bottled vinaigrette salad dressing
- 1 hard-cooked egg, finely chopped
- 1/4 cup crumbled cooked bacon

In large bowl, combine spinach, mushrooms, onion, avocado, tuna and dressing; toss gently. Sprinkle with egg and bacon.

Makes 6 servings

Prep Time: 20 minutes

Marinated Albacore and Mushroom Salad with Quick Sour Cream Dressing

Albacore Salad Tropicale

A light and refreshing salad, great for a picnic.

- **1 fresh pineapple, halved *or* 1 can (8¼ ounces) crushed pineapple, drain juice and reserve**
- **2 cups cooked elbow, shells or salad macaroni**
- **1 can (8 ounces) water chestnuts, drained and sliced**
- **½ cup chopped red bell pepper**
- **½ cup sliced green onions, including tops**
- **1 cup Tropicale Dressing (recipe follows)**
- **1 can (6 ounces) StarKist Solid White Tuna, drained and chunked**
- **4 cups chopped romaine lettuce (optional)**
- **8 cherry tomatoes, halved, for garnish**

Hollow out pineapple halves to about ¾ inch from edge. Core and finely chop pineapple; reserve one cup for salad. Refrigerate remaining pineapple for another use.

Combine macaroni, reserved pineapple, water chestnuts, red pepper and onions. Toss with Tropicale Dressing; refrigerate several hours. Just before serving, add tuna; toss gently. Serve salad from pineapple halves or over lettuce. Garnish with tomatoes.

Makes 4 servings

Tropicale Dressing

- **¼ cup juice reserved from canned crushed pineapple or canned pineapple juice**
- **2 tablespoons lemon juice**
- **1 teaspoon garlic salt**
- **½ teaspoon sugar**
- **½ teaspoon lemon pepper seasoning**
- **½ teaspoon paprika**
- **½ cup olive oil**

Whisk together pineapple juice, lemon juice, garlic salt, sugar, lemon pepper seasoning and paprika. Slowly add oil, whisking continuously, until well blended.

Prep Time: 15 minutes

Albacore Salad Tropicale

Easy Tossed Niçoise with Garlic and Cheese Dressing

You will love the ease with which this salad comes together. All the flavors of the classic without a lot of fuss.

1½ pounds steamed red potatoes, cut into small chunks
1 package (10 ounces) frozen Italian green beans, thawed and drained
¾ cup niçoise or pitted ripe olives, sliced
½ red onion, slivered
½ red bell pepper, slivered
½ green bell pepper, slivered
¼ cup coarsely chopped green onions, including tops
1½ cups Garlic and Cheese Dressing (recipe follows)
1 can (12 ounces) StarKist Solid White Tuna, drained and chunked
½ cup minced fresh parsley
Whole romaine leaves, washed and dried
Freshly ground black pepper (optional)
Grated Parmesan cheese (optional)

In large bowl, combine potatoes, beans, olives, red onion, bell peppers and green onions; toss with Garlic and Cheese Dressing. Refrigerate. Just before serving, add tuna and parsley. Line plates with lettuce; spoon salad onto leaves. Serve with black pepper and cheese, if desired.

Makes 6 to 8 servings

Garlic and Cheese Dressing

¼ cup wine vinegar
2 tablespoons lemon juice
1 to 2 cloves garlic, minced or pressed
1 tablespoon Dijon-style mustard
Salt and pepper to taste
1 cup olive oil
½ cup grated Parmesan cheese

In small bowl, whisk together vinegar, lemon juice, garlic, mustard, salt and pepper. Slowly add olive oil, whisking until all oil is added and dressing is thickened. Stir in cheese.

Prep Time: 15 minutes

Tuna, Tomato and Cucumber Salad

Enjoy the refreshing combination of ingredients this recipe offers.

4 cups shredded lettuce: romaine, red leaf, butter or wild baby greens
4 plum tomatoes, sliced
½ cucumber, sliced
1 can (2¼ ounces) sliced ripe olives, drained
1 can (12 ounces) StarKist Solid White Tuna, drained and chunked
1 cup Lemon Yogurt with Dill Dressing or Tangy Horseradish Dressing (recipes follow)
1 tablespoon minced fresh parsley
1 cup toasted sourdough croutons

For *each* salad on chilled plate, arrange 1 cup lettuce; top with ¼ *each* of tomatoes, cucumber, olives and tuna; drizzle Lemon Yogurt with Dill Dressing or Tangy Horseradish Dressing over salad. Sprinkle with parsley and croutons. Serve immediately. Serve extra dressing on the side.   *Makes 4 servings*

Lemon Yogurt with Dill Dressing

  ½ cup plain yogurt
  ¼ cup light mayonnaise
  2 tablespoons lemon or lime juice
1½ to 2 tablespoons dried dill weed
  1 tablespoon white wine vinegar
  ¼ teaspoon salt
  ¼ teaspoon freshly ground black pepper

In small bowl, combine all ingredients; blend until smooth and creamy. Chill several hours before serving.

Tangy Horseradish Dressing

  ½ cup light mayonnaise
  ¼ cup plus 2 tablespoons red wine vinegar
  ¼ cup plain nonfat yogurt
  2 tablespoons minced fresh parsley
  1 to 2 tablespoons Dijon-style mustard
  ½ to 1 tablespoon prepared horseradish
  ½ teaspoon salt
  ¼ teaspoon paprika

In small bowl, combine all ingredients; blend until smooth and creamy. Chill several hours before serving.

Prep Time: 12 minutes

Mediterranean Pasta Salad

Serve this garlic lovers' salad at room temperature with hot crusty bread.

  4 cups cooked and cooled penne
  1 pound plum tomatoes, peeled and coarsely chopped
  1 can (12 ounces) StarKist Solid White Tuna, drained and chunked
  1 jar (6 ounces) marinated artichoke hearts, drained and coarsely chopped
  1 can (4¼ ounces) chopped ripe olives, drained
  ½ cup grated Parmesan cheese
  2 tablespoons drained capers, minced
  1 to 2 teaspoons minced fresh garlic
  ¼ cup lemon juice
  2 tablespoons red wine vinegar
  ⅓ cup olive oil
  1 teaspoon dried oregano, crushed
  ½ teaspoon lemon pepper seasoning
    Salt and black pepper to taste
    Additional grated Parmesan cheese

In large bowl, combine penne, tomatoes, tuna, artichoke hearts, olives, ½ cup cheese, capers and garlic; toss gently. In small bowl, combine lemon juice, vinegar, oil, oregano, lemon pepper seasoning, salt and pepper; whisk to blend well. Toss tuna mixture with dressing; sprinkle with additional cheese, if desired.   *Makes 6 to 8 servings*

Prep Time: 15 minutes

Fruity Brown Rice Salad with Raspberry Vinaigrette

This is an easy recipe to halve or double.

  2 cups cooked brown rice
  2 cups small broccoli flowerets, blanched and chilled
  2 cups fresh or canned pineapple chunks
  1 can (11 ounces) mandarin oranges, drained
  ½ cup slivered red bell pepper
  ½ cup chopped red onion
    Raspberry Vinaigrette Dressing (recipe follows)
  1 can (12 ounces) StarKist Solid White Tuna, drained and chunked
  6 to 8 Bibb lettuce cups

In large bowl, mix together rice, broccoli, pineapple, oranges, red pepper and onion. Add Raspberry Vinaigrette Dressing; toss. Refrigerate several hours before serving. Just before serving, add tuna; toss gently. Serve in lettuce cups.   *Makes 6 to 8 servings*

Raspberry Vinaigrette Dressing

  ¼ cup raspberry vinegar or apple cider vinegar
  2 tablespoons orange or lemon juice
  1 tablespoon brown sugar
  1 teaspoon seasoned salt
  ½ teaspoon crushed red pepper
  1 medium clove garlic, finely minced or pressed
  ½ cup olive oil

In small bowl, whisk together vinegar, orange juice, brown sugar, seasoned salt, crushed red pepper and garlic. Slowly add oil, whisking continuously until well blended.

Prep Time: 15 minutes

Oriental Albacore Salad

Try an Oriental-flavored bottled dressing to complement this salad.

  1 can (12 ounces) StarKist Solid White Tuna, drained and chunked
  1 cup bean sprouts
  ½ cup sliced celery
  ⅓ cup sliced green onions, including tops
  1 can (11 ounces) mandarin oranges, drained
  ½ to ¾ cup bottled Oriental salad dressing
  4 to 5 cups salad greens, romaine, iceberg, purple cabbage, savoy cabbage and bok choy
  ½ cup crisp chow mein noodles or chopped cashews

In large bowl, combine tuna, bean sprouts, celery, onions, oranges and dressing; toss gently. Add salad greens; toss again. Top each serving with chow mein noodles.
                  Makes 6 servings

Prep Time: 15 minutes

Fruity Brown Rice Salad with Raspberry Vinaigrette

Tuna Louie Salad

A colorful, delectable salad with a variation on Thousand Island dressing that you'll adore.

>   Bibb lettuce
> 1 can (12 ounces) StarKist Solid
>   White Tuna, drained and
>   chunked
> 2 avocados, sliced
> 2 to 4 hard-cooked eggs, sliced
> 4 plum tomatoes, sliced
> 16 ounces canned grapefruit
>   sections, drained and juice
>   reserved
> 1/3 cup whipping cream, whipped
> 1/2 cup Thousand Island dressing
>   Lime wedges, for garnish

On four serving plates, arrange lettuce, tuna, avocados, eggs, tomatoes and grapefruit. In small bowl, fold whipped cream into Thousand Island dressing. For thinner dressing, add 1 to 2 tablespoons reserved grapefruit juice. Spoon dressing over salads or serve separately. Garnish with lime wedges.   *Makes 4 servings*

Prep Time: 8 minutes

Albacore and Mandarin Orange Salad with Caramelized Almonds

Almonds can be caramelized in 2 1/2 minutes.

> 2 teaspoons vegetable oil
> 1/3 to 1/2 cup blanched slivered
>   almonds (2-ounce package)
> 1/4 cup sugar
>   Bibb lettuce
> 1 can (6 ounces) StarKist Solid
>   White Tuna, drained and
>   chunked
> 2 cans (11 ounces *each*)
>   mandarin oranges, drained
> 1/2 cup sliced red onion
> 1/2 cup dried cranberries
>   (optional)
> 1/3 cup bottled sesame-flavored or
>   vinaigrette dressing

Spray 14-inch sheet of foil with nonstick cooking spray. In heavy 2-quart saucepan, heat oil over medium-high heat until hot. Add almonds; stir constantly with wooden spoon 30 to 45 seconds or until nuts begin to turn golden. Add sugar; lower heat to medium. Continue cooking and stirring 1 to 1 1/2 more minutes or until sugar is caramelized and golden brown. Pour out onto foil, separating nuts. Cool 5 minutes while preparing salad; break nuts into pieces.

On individual plates, arrange lettuce, tuna, oranges, onion and cranberries, if desired. Drizzle with dressing; sprinkle with caramelized almonds.   *Makes 4 servings*

Prep Time: 12 minutes

Tuna Louie Salad

Tuna Pasta Primavera Salad

This salad is chock-full of garden vegetables. Don't hesitate to use any fresh vegetables you have.

   2 cups cooked and chilled small
      shell pasta
1 1/2 cups halved cherry tomatoes
   1/2 cup thinly sliced carrots
   1/2 cup sliced celery
   1/2 cup chopped seeded peeled
      cucumber
   1/2 cup thinly sliced radishes
   1/2 cup thawed frozen peas
   1/4 cup slivered red bell pepper
   2 tablespoons minced green
      onion, including tops
   1 can (12 ounces) StarKist Solid
      White or Chunk Light Tuna,
      drained and chunked
   1 cup salad dressing of choice
      Bibb or red leaf lettuce
      Fresh herbs, for garnish

In large bowl, combine all ingredients except lettuce and herbs. Chill several hours. If using oil and vinegar dressing, stir salad mixture occasionally to evenly marinate ingredients. Place lettuce leaves on each plate; spoon on salad. Garnish with fresh herbs, if desired.

Makes 6 servings

Prep Time: 25 minutes

Sunshine Albacore and Orange Salad

Here we combine oranges and grapes for a refreshing salad.

   2 oranges, peeled
   1 can (6 ounces) StarKist Solid
      White Tuna, drained and
      chunked
   1 cup chopped Belgian endive
   1 cup seedless green grape
      halves
   1/4 cup thinly sliced purple
      cabbage
      Sunshine Dressing (recipe
      follows)
      Lettuce leaves
   2 tablespoons slivered almonds,
      toasted

Slice oranges crosswise into rounds; cut rounds into quarters. In medium bowl, combine oranges with tuna, endive, grapes and cabbage. Toss with Sunshine Dressing; serve on lettuce leaves. Sprinkle each serving with almonds.

Makes 2 servings

Sunshine Dressing
   1/2 cup plain yogurt
   2 tablespoons mayonnaise
   2 to 3 tablespoons orange juice
   1 to 1 1/2 teaspoons orange peel
   1/8 teaspoon paprika
      Salt to taste

In small bowl, combine all ingredients; blend well.

Prep Time: 10 minutes

Tuna Pasta Primavera Salad

Sensational

❖❖❖

SAUCES

Ricotta Green Chiles and Albacore Sauce

You will love the rich taste of this sauce made with low fat dairy products.

  1 egg, lightly beaten
  1 cup (8 ounces) reduced fat
      ricotta cheese
  1 cup low fat milk
  ¼ cup grated Parmesan cheese
  2 tablespoons diced green chiles
  1 jar (2 ounces) sliced or diced
      pimiento, drained
  ½ teaspoon garlic salt
  ½ teaspoon ground black pepper
  1 can (6 ounces) StarKist Solid
      White Tuna, drained and
      chunked
  2 cups hot cooked rice

In 1½-quart saucepan, combine all ingredients except tuna and rice; blend well. Heat thoroughly over low heat. Add tuna and rice; heat 1 more minute.   *Makes 4 servings*

Note: For a spicier sauce, substitute fresh roasted and chopped Anaheim chiles for the green chiles.

Prep Time: 15 minutes

Creamy Tuna Broccoli and Swiss Sauce

Enjoy this special and easy-to-prepare dish at home.

  1 can (10¾ ounces) cream of
      broccoli soup
  ½ cup half & half
  ½ cup shredded Swiss cheese
  2 cups chopped cooked
      broccoli*
  1 jar (2 ounces) sliced pimiento,
      drained
  1 can (6 ounces) StarKist Solid
      White or Chunk Light Tuna,
      drained and chunked
  Hot cooked pasta or rice

In medium saucepan, combine soup, half & half and cheese; cook over low heat, stirring to blend well. Stir in broccoli, pimiento and tuna; continue cooking until sauce is thoroughly heated. Serve over pasta.
          Makes 2 servings

*Or substitute 1 package (10 ounces) frozen broccoli cuts, cooked and drained.

Prep Time: 15 minutes

Creamy Tuna Broccoli and Swiss Sauce

Tuna and Caponata Sauce

This savory tuna and vegetable sauce is great tossed with hot pasta.

   Olive oil
 2 cups diced, peeled eggplant
 1/2 cup chopped onion
 1/2 cup chopped celery
 1/2 cup coarsely grated carrot
 1/4 pound mushrooms, chopped
 1 can (14 1/2 ounces) Italian
      pasta-style tomatoes*
 1 can (6 ounces) StarKist Solid
      White or Chunk Light Tuna,
      drained and flaked
   Salt and pepper to taste
   Hot cooked pasta

In 3-quart saucepan, heat several tablespoons olive oil over medium-high heat; sauté 1/3 of eggplant until browned. Remove from pan; set aside. Repeat until all eggplant is browned and reserved. Heat several tablespoons oil; sauté onion, celery, carrot and mushrooms until onion is tender. Return eggplant to saucepan; stir in tomatoes and tuna. Simmer about 15 minutes; add salt and pepper. Serve over pasta.

Makes 4 servings

*Or substitute 1 can (14 1/2 ounces) cut-up tomatoes, 1/2 teaspoon minced or pressed garlic and 1 teaspoon Italian herb seasoning.

Note: This recipe is easily doubled.

Prep Time: 25 minutes

Creamy Tuna Spinach and Ricotta Sauce

Almost a meal in itself, but plan to serve this delicious sauce over toasted French rolls or steamed rice.

 2 tablespoons butter or
      margarine
 1 package (10 ounces) frozen
      chopped spinach, thawed
      and squeezed dry
 2 tablespoons diced green chiles
 1/2 to 1 teaspoon minced or
      pressed fresh garlic
 2 eggs, lightly beaten
1 1/4 cups half & half
 1 cup (8 ounces) ricotta cheese
 1/4 cup grated Parmesan cheese
 3/4 teaspoon seasoned salt
 1/2 teaspoon ground black pepper
 1/2 teaspoon dried thyme, crushed
 1 can (12 ounces) StarKist Solid
      White or Chunk Light Tuna,
      drained and chunked
 3 French rolls, halved and
      toasted or steamed rice

In heavy 1 1/2-quart saucepan, melt butter over medium heat; sauté spinach, chiles and garlic. In bowl, combine eggs, half & half, ricotta, Parmesan cheese and seasonings. Add ricotta mixture to sautéed spinach; blend well. Cook over medium heat until sauce begins to thicken. Add tuna; continue cooking until tuna is thoroughly heated. Serve over French rolls.

Makes 6 servings

Prep Time: 20 minutes

Tuna and Caponata Sauce

StarKist Garden Albacore Sauce

This vegetable and Swiss cheese sauce is perfect over pasta or rice.

  2 cups chicken broth
  1 package (1.8 ounces) white sauce mix
  1 cup shredded Swiss cheese
  1 can (6 ounces) StarKist Solid White Tuna, drained and chunked
  1 cup sliced mushrooms
  1 cup sliced bell pepper, green, red and/or yellow
  1 cup sliced green beans, blanched
  ½ teaspoon seasoned pepper blend
  Hot cooked pasta or rice

In 1½-quart saucepan, combine chicken broth and white sauce mix; blend with wire whisk. Cook over medium-high heat, whisking constantly, until sauce thickens. Reduce heat to low; add Swiss cheese, stirring until melted. Add tuna, mushrooms, bell peppers, green beans and pepper blend; heat thoroughly. Serve over pasta.

Makes 4 servings

Prep Time: 20 minutes

Creamy Cilantro and Chile Sauce

This sauce is excellent over rice, pasta or toasted cornbread.

  1 cup coarsely chopped onion
  ½ cup fresh cilantro leaves
  1 can (7 ounces) whole green chiles, seeded
  1 to 2 cloves garlic
  1 tablespoon dried oregano
  ½ teaspoon ground cumin
  ¼ teaspoon salt
  1 cup shredded Monterey Jack cheese
  1 can (6 ounces) StarKist Solid White Tuna, drained
  ½ cup sour cream
  Toasted cornbread, hot cooked rice or pasta
  1 tablespoon toasted sesame seeds, for garnish

In food processor bowl with metal blade, combine onion, cilantro, chiles and garlic; process until smooth and thick. Transfer mixture to 1-quart saucepan. Add oregano, cumin and salt; heat over low heat, stirring frequently. Just before serving, stir in cheese, tuna and sour cream, stirring just until heated and cheese is melted *(do not boil)*. Serve immediately over cornbread. Garnish with sesame seeds.

Makes 4 servings

Note: For a more piquant flavor, substitute fresh roasted Anaheim chiles for the canned mild green chiles.

Prep Time: 15 minutes

StarKist Garden Albacore Sauce

Prime-Time

❖❖❖

TEMPTATIONS

Homestyle Tuna Pot Pie

Making a pot pie has never been easier.

 1 package (15 ounces)
    refrigerated pie crusts
 1 can (12 ounces) StarKist Solid
    White or Chunk Light Tuna,
    drained and chunked
 1 package (10 ounces) frozen
    peas and carrots, thawed
    and drained
½ cup chopped onion
 1 can (10¾ ounces) cream of
    potato or cream of
    mushroom soup
⅓ cup milk
½ teaspoon poultry seasoning or
    dried thyme, crushed
    Salt and pepper to taste

Line 9-inch pie pan with one crust; set aside. Reserve second crust. In medium bowl, combine remaining ingredients; mix well. Pour tuna mixture into pie shell; top with second crust. Crimp edges to seal. Cut slits in top crust to vent. Bake in 375°F oven 45 to 50 minutes or until golden brown.

Makes 6 servings

Prep Time: 55 to 60 minutes

Sesame Almond Rice Dinner

This Indian dish's sweet raisins and hot chili complement the tuna and rice.

 1 tablespoon sesame oil
 1 teaspoon minced or pressed
    fresh garlic
⅓ cup slivered almonds
 1 cup long grain white rice
¾ cup golden raisins
 1 to 1½ teaspoons chili powder
 2 cups chicken broth
 1 can (6 ounces) StarKist Solid
    White Tuna, drained and
    chunked

In 1½-quart saucepan with tight-fitting lid, heat oil over medium-high heat. Add garlic, almonds and rice; sauté until golden. Stir in raisins, chili powder and chicken broth. Bring to a boil; cover. Reduce heat; simmer about 20 minutes or until rice has absorbed all liquid. Stir in tuna; serve. *Makes 4 servings*

Tip: Serve with steamed broccoli spears and chutney.

Prep Time: 30 minutes

Homestyle Tuna Pot Pie

Spicy Tuna and Linguine with Garlic and Pine Nuts

A great meal-in-a-dish that impresses company and uses only one pan.

  2 tablespoons olive oil
  4 cloves garlic, minced
  2 cups sliced mushrooms
  ½ cup chopped onion
  ½ teaspoon crushed red pepper
2½ cups chopped plum tomatoes
  1 can (14½ ounces) chicken broth *plus* water to equal 2 cups
  ½ teaspoon salt
  ¼ teaspoon coarsely ground black pepper
  1 package (9 ounces) uncooked fresh linguine
  1 can (12 ounces) StarKist Solid White Tuna, drained and chunked
  ⅓ cup chopped fresh cilantro
  ⅓ cup toasted pine nuts or almonds

In 12-inch skillet, heat olive oil over medium-high heat; sauté garlic, mushrooms, onion and red pepper until golden brown. Add tomatoes, chicken broth mixture, salt and black pepper; bring to a boil.

Separate uncooked linguine into strands; place in skillet and spoon sauce over. Reduce heat to simmer; cook, covered, 4 more minutes or until cooked through. Toss gently; add tuna and cilantro and toss again. Sprinkle with pine nuts.
Makes 4 to 6 servings

Prep Time: 12 minutes

Creamy Scalloped Potatoes and Tuna

What a fabulous way to cook potatoes and tuna!

  2 cups milk
  2 cups whipping cream
  2 cloves garlic, minced
2½ pounds (about 6 medium) white or russet potatoes
  ¾ teaspoon salt
  ½ teaspoon white pepper
  1 tablespoon butter or margarine
  1 can (12 ounces) StarKist Solid White or Chunk Light Tuna, drained and chunked
1½ cups shredded mozzarella cheese

In 3-quart saucepan over medium heat, heat milk, cream and garlic while preparing potatoes. Peel potatoes; slice about ⅛ to ¼ inch thick. Add potatoes, salt and white pepper to milk mixture; heat to simmering.

Grease 11×7-inch casserole with butter; spoon potato-milk mixture into dish. Bake 25 minutes; remove from oven. Add tuna, stirring gently; top with cheese. Bake 35 more minutes or until potatoes are cooked through and top is golden brown. Let stand, covered, about 15 minutes to thicken.   *Makes 6 to 8 servings*

Prep Time: 70 minutes

Spicy Tuna and Linguine with Garlic and Pine Nuts

Easy Three Cheese Tuna Soufflé

This is a great do-ahead dish for the entire family.

    4 cups large croutons*
2½ cups milk
    4 large eggs
    1 can (10¾ ounces) cream of
        celery soup
    3 cups shredded cheese, use a
        combination of Cheddar,
        Monterey Jack and Swiss
    1 can (12 ounces) StarKist Solid
        White or Chunk Light Tuna,
        drained and flaked
    1 tablespoon butter or margarine
½ cup chopped celery
½ cup finely chopped onion
¼ pound mushrooms, sliced

In bottom of lightly greased 13×9-inch baking dish, arrange croutons. In medium bowl, beat together milk, eggs and soup; stir in cheeses and tuna. In small skillet, melt butter over medium heat. Add celery, onion and mushrooms; sauté until onion is soft.

Spoon sautéed vegetables over croutons; pour egg-tuna mixture over top. Cover; refrigerate overnight. Remove from refrigerator 1 hour before baking; bake in 325°F oven 45 to 50 minutes or until hot and bubbly.   *Makes 8 servings*

*Use garlic and herb or ranch-flavored croutons.

Prep Time: 60 minutes

Tuna Manicotti in Creamy Dill Sauce

This traditional dish is seasoned with a light, lemony dill sauce.

    2 tablespoons butter or
        margarine
¼ cup chopped onion
¼ cup chopped celery
¾ cup chopped mushrooms
¼ cup grated Parmesan cheese
    3 tablespoons mayonnaise
1½ cups Quick White Sauce,
        divided (page 76)
    3 tablespoons lemon juice
    1 tablespoon dried dill weed
        Salt and pepper to taste
    1 can (12 ounces) StarKist Solid
        White or Chunk Light Tuna,
        drained and flaked
    6 manicotti shells, cooked
        al dente, rinsed and drained
½ cup shredded mozzarella
        cheese

In small saucepan, melt butter over medium heat; sauté onion, celery and mushrooms until onion is soft; cool. In large bowl, combine Parmesan cheese, mayonnaise, ¾ cup white sauce, lemon juice, dill, salt and pepper; blend well. Stir in tuna and sautéed vegetables; blend well.

Carefully stuff manicotti shells; arrange in baking dish. Pour remaining ¾ cup white sauce over stuffed manicotti; sprinkle mozzarella cheese over sauce. Bake in 350°F oven 30 minutes or until heated through.
          Makes 4 to 6 servings

Prep Time: 45 minutes

Easy Three Cheese Tuna Soufflé

Thai-Style Tuna Fried Rice

Aficionados of Thai food will appreciate this simple dish.

Vegetable oil
2 eggs, lightly beaten
2/3 cup uncooked peeled medium shrimp chopped into 3/4-inch pieces
3 cloves garlic
1 to 2 tablespoons minced fresh serrano chiles
4 to 6 cups cooked rice, chilled overnight
1 tablespoon sugar
1 tablespoon nam pla (fish sauce) (optional)
1 tablespoon soy sauce
1 can (6 ounces) StarKist Solid White or Chunk Light Tuna, drained and chunked
1/2 cup chopped dry-roasted peanuts
1/4 cup chopped fresh basil
2 tablespoons chopped fresh cilantro
Lime wedges, for garnish

In wok, heat 1 tablespoon oil over medium-high heat; add eggs and cook lightly, stirring, until partially cooked but still runny. Return eggs to bowl. Wipe out wok with paper towels. Add 2 tablespoons oil to wok; heat.

Add shrimp, garlic and chiles. Stir-fry until shrimp turn pink, about 3 minutes. Remove shrimp; set aside. Add 1 or 2 tablespoons oil to wok; stir-fry rice, sugar, nam pla, if desired and soy sauce until rice is heated through. Add tuna and peanuts; heat.

Return shrimp and eggs to pan, chopping eggs into pieces with stir-fry spatula. Add basil and cilantro; toss gently to mix. Serve with lime wedges for garnish; squeeze juice on fried rice, if desired.

Makes 4 to 6 servings

Prep Time: 15 minutes

Albacore Quiche

Serve this impressive looking egg-cheese dish at your next brunch.

1 (9-inch) pie shell *or* 1 refrigerated (1/2 of 15-ounce package) pie crust
1 can (6 ounces) StarKist Solid White Tuna, drained and flaked
1/3 cup chopped green onions
3/4 cup shredded Cheddar or Swiss cheese or a combination of cheeses
3 large eggs
1 1/4 cups half & half or milk
1/2 teaspoon dried basil or dill weed
1/4 teaspoon ground black pepper

Line pie shell with foil; fill with pie weights, dry beans or rice. Bake in 375°F oven 10 minutes. Remove foil and pie weights; place tuna, onions and cheese in pie shell. In medium bowl, combine eggs, half & half and seasonings; pour over pie shell. Continue baking 40 to 50 more minutes or until quiche is set and knife inserted near center comes out clean. Cool slightly before serving.

Makes 6 servings

Prep Time: 60 minutes

Thai-Style Tuna Fried Rice

Tuna Puffs with Tomato-Orange Salsa

These tuna puffs bake quickly in muffin pans.

> 2 large eggs
> ¾ cup coarsely crushed cheese cracker crumbs
> ¼ cup evaporated milk
> 2 tablespoons melted butter
> 1 tablespoon lemon juice
> 1 teaspoon ground cumin
> ¼ to ½ teaspoon liquid red pepper
> 1 can (12 ounces) StarKist Solid White or Chunk Light Tuna, drained and chunked
> ⅓ cup minced green onions, including tops
> Salt and pepper to taste
> Quick Tomato-Orange Salsa or Fresh Tomato-Orange Salsa (recipes follow)

In medium bowl, beat eggs with whisk; blend in crumbs, milk, butter, lemon juice, cumin and liquid red pepper; blend. Add tuna, onions, salt and pepper.

Spray 6 (2½-inch) muffin cups with cooking spray. Divide tuna mixture among cups. Bake in 375°F oven 20 to 25 minutes or until toothpick inserted near center comes out clean. Prepare desired salsa recipe. Serve Tuna Puffs with Quick Tomato-Orange Salsa or Fresh Tomato-Orange Salsa.

Makes 6 servings

Tip: Crush crackers in plastic bag with rolling pin.

Quick Tomato-Orange Salsa

> ½ cup thick and chunky salsa
> 1 tablespoon frozen orange juice concentrate

In small bowl, stir salsa and orange juice concentrate together. Serve with Tuna Puffs. Refrigerate leftovers.

Fresh Tomato-Orange Salsa

> ½ cup plum tomatoes chopped in ¼-inch pieces
> ½ cup oranges or mandarin oranges chopped in ½-inch pieces
> 2 tablespoons red onion chopped in ¼-inch pieces
> 2 tablespoons chopped fresh cilantro
> 1 to 2 tablespoons minced serrano chiles

In small bowl, gently mix all ingredients together. Serve with Tuna Puffs. Refrigerate leftovers.

Prep Time: 45 minutes

Tuna Puffs with Tomato-Orange Salsa

Tuna and Broccoli Bake

Enjoy this quick and easy-to-prepare light tuna and broccoli dish.

- **1 package (16 ounces) frozen broccoli cuts, thawed and well drained**
- **2 slices bread, cut in ½-inch cubes**
- **1 can (12 ounces) StarKist Solid White or Chunk Light Tuna, drained and chunked**
- **3 eggs**
- **2 cups cottage cheese**
- **1 cup shredded Cheddar cheese**
- **¼ teaspoon ground black pepper**

Place broccoli on bottom of 2-quart baking dish. Top with bread cubes and tuna. In medium bowl, combine eggs, cottage cheese, Cheddar cheese and pepper. Spread evenly over tuna mixture. Bake in 400°F oven 30 minutes or until golden brown and puffed.

Makes 4 servings

Prep Time: 35 minutes

Herbed Rice and Creamy Corn

The sweet creamed corn and bell peppers harmonize with the savory herbs and rice.

- **1 cup long grain white rice**
- **1 can (14½ ounces) chicken broth**
- **½ teaspoon garlic powder**
- **¼ teaspoon dried thyme, crushed**
- **¼ teaspoon dried oregano, crushed**
- **1 can (17 ounces) cream-style corn**
- **½ cup chopped green bell pepper**
- **½ cup chopped red bell pepper**
- **1 can (12 ounces) StarKist Solid White or Chunk Light Tuna, drained and chunked**

In 1½-quart saucepan with tight-fitting lid, combine rice, chicken broth, garlic powder, thyme and oregano. Bring to a boil; cover. Reduce heat; simmer about 15 minutes. Stir in corn and bell peppers; cover. Continue cooking 5 to 8 more minutes or until rice is tender. Stir in tuna.

Makes 4 servings

Prep Time: 25 minutes

Tuna and Broccoli Bake

Main-Dish

♦♦♦

MAGIC

Albacore Stir-Fry

Enjoy the flavors of the Orient with this easy-to-prepare stir-fry.

   3 tablespoons vegetable oil
½ cup sliced onion
   1 clove garlic, minced or pressed
   1 bag (16 ounces) frozen
      Oriental vegetables, thawed
      and drained*
   1 can (12 ounces) StarKist Solid
      White Tuna, drained and
      chunked
   3 tablespoons soy sauce
   1 tablespoon lemon juice
   1 tablespoon water
   1 teaspoon sugar
   2 cups hot cooked rice

In wok or large skillet, heat oil over medium-high heat; sauté onion and garlic until onion is soft. Add vegetables; cook about 3 to 4 minutes or until vegetables are crisp-tender. Add tuna, soy sauce, lemon juice, water and sugar. Cook 1 more minute; serve over rice.

Makes 4 servings

*May use 4 cups fresh vegetables, such as carrots, peapods, broccoli, bell peppers, mushrooms, celery and bean sprouts.

Prep Time: 20 minutes

Tuna Cakes

This is a quick and easy version of a classic seafood dish.

1¼ cups breadcrumbs, divided
   1 can (12 ounces) StarKist Solid
      White or Chunk Light Tuna,
      drained and flaked
¾ cup shredded Cheddar cheese
¼ cup mayonnaise
   1 egg, lightly beaten
⅓ cup bottled ranch dressing
½ cup finely chopped onion
½ cup finely chopped red or
      green bell pepper (optional)
   2 tablespoons vegetable oil,
      divided

In large bowl, combine ½ cup breadcrumbs with remaining ingredients except oil. Shape mixture into 8 patties, coating with remaining breadcrumbs. In nonstick skillet, heat 1 tablespoon oil over medium heat; cook 4 tuna cakes about 3 minutes per side. Repeat cooking process with remaining 1 tablespoon oil and 4 tuna cakes.

Makes 4 servings

Prep Time: 25 minutes

Albacore Stir-Fry

Baked Potatoes with Tuna and Broccoli in Cheese Sauce

With a microwave, this is an almost instant dinner-winner.

- **2 medium baking potatoes (6 to 8 ounces *each*)**
- **1 package (10 ounces) frozen broccoli in cheese sauce**
- **1 can (6 ounces) StarKist Solid White Tuna, drained and chunked**
- **1 teaspoon chili powder**
- **¼ cup minced green onions, including tops**
- **2 slices cooked, crumbled bacon**

Microwave Directions: Wash and pierce potatoes; microwave on HIGH 8 minutes. Wrap in foil; let stand to finish cooking while preparing broccoli. Microwave vented pouch of broccoli on HIGH 5 minutes. In medium microwaveable bowl, combine tuna and chili powder. Gently stir in broccoli. Cover; heat on HIGH 1½ more minutes or until heated through. Cut potatoes in half lengthwise. Top with broccoli-tuna mixture; sprinkle with onions and bacon.   *Makes 2 servings*

Note: Recipe can easily be doubled for 4 — just cook a little longer in the microwave.

Prep Time: 20 minutes

Curried Tuna Shells

Curry used to be considered an exotic seasoning. Today, curry is used in all types of dishes to create a unique flavor. Young children will give this rave reviews.

- **1 to 2 tablespoons vegetable oil**
- **½ cup chopped onion**
- **½ cup chopped red bell pepper**
- **1 medium zucchini, chopped**
- **2 cups Quick White Sauce (recipe follows)**
- **1½ teaspoons curry powder**
- **1 can (6 ounces) StarKist Solid White or Chunk Light Tuna, drained and flaked**
- **6 ounces large pasta shells, cooked according to package directions**

In large skillet, heat oil over medium-high heat; sauté onion and bell pepper until onion is soft. Add zucchini; sauté 2 more minutes. In large saucepan, combine white sauce with curry powder; blend well. Stir in tuna, cooked pasta and sautéed vegetables. Heat thoroughly; serve.
Makes 4 servings

Quick White Sauce: In small saucepan, mix together 1 package (1.8 ounces) white sauce mix, 1½ cups milk or half & half and ¾ cup chicken broth. Bring to a boil over medium heat, stirring constantly. Reduce heat; cook 1 more minute, stirring constantly.

Prep Time: 20 minutes

Baked Potatoes with Tuna and Broccoli in Cheese Sauce

StarKist Garden Spaghetti

This light, lemony sauce complements the tuna and vegetables.

    ½ pound whole wheat spaghetti
    2 tablespoons butter or
        margarine
    1 small onion, sliced
    ¼ pound mushrooms, sliced
    2 cups chicken or vegetable
        broth
    2 tablespoons flour
    2 tablespoons lemon juice
    2 tablespoons drained chopped
        pimiento
    1 teaspoon grated lemon peel
    1 teaspoon dried thyme, crushed
    ¼ teaspoon garlic powder
        Salt and pepper to taste
    1 can (12 ounces) StarKist Solid
        White or Chunk Light Tuna,
        drained and chunked
    2 cups cooked sliced carrots
    2 cups cooked broccoli flowerets
        Tomato wedges, for garnish

Cook spaghetti according to package directions; drain, rinse and keep warm over medium-high heat. In large skillet, melt butter over medium heat; sauté onion 2 to 3 minutes. Add mushrooms; continue cooking 1 to 2 minutes.

In medium bowl, combine broth, flour, lemon juice, pimiento, lemon peel, thyme, garlic powder, salt and pepper. Add to onion-mushroom mixture; cook about 5 minutes over medium-high heat or until slightly thickened. Stir in tuna, carrots and broccoli; heat. Gently toss with spaghetti. Serve with tomato, if desired.   *Makes 6 servings*

Prep Time: 25 minutes

StarKist Swiss Potato Pie

Easy enough for kids to make and definitely family pleasing. This may be assembled in the morning and cooked that evening.

    1 cup milk
    4 large eggs, beaten
    4 cups frozen shredded hash
        brown potatoes, thawed
    2 cups shredded Swiss cheese
    ½ to 1 cup chopped green
        onions, including tops
    ½ cup sour cream
    ½ cup chopped green bell pepper
        (optional)
    ½ teaspoon garlic powder
    1 can (6 ounces) StarKist Solid
        White Tuna, drained and
        flaked

In large bowl, combine all ingredients. Pour into lightly greased deep 10-inch pie plate. Bake in 350°F oven 1 hour and 20 minutes or until golden and crusty. Let stand a few minutes before slicing into serving portions.

Makes 6 servings

Prep Time: 90 minutes

StarKist Garden Spaghetti

Biscuit-Topped Tuna Bake

This recipe is a real family pleaser. For a fun look, snip each biscuit into fourths before placing on top of the casserole.

  2 tablespoons vegetable oil
½ cup chopped onion
½ cup chopped celery
  1 can (12 ounces) StarKist Solid
     White or Chunk Light Tuna,
     drained and chunked
  1 can (10¾ ounces) cream of
     potato soup
  1 package (10 ounces) frozen
     peas and carrots, thawed
¾ cup milk
¼ teaspoon ground black pepper
¼ teaspoon garlic powder
  1 can (7½ ounces) refrigerator
     flaky biscuits

In large skillet, heat oil over medium-high heat; sauté onion and celery until onion is soft. Add remaining ingredients except biscuits; heat thoroughly. Transfer mixture to 1½-quart casserole. Arrange biscuits around top edge of dish; bake in 400°F oven 10 to 15 minutes or until biscuits are golden brown. *Makes 4 to 6 servings*

Prep Time: 25 minutes

Albacore and Asparagus Pasta

This simple recipe's rich taste will really surprise you.

½ pound uncooked angel hair
     pasta
  1 tablespoon olive oil
  1 can (10¾ ounces) cream of
     asparagus soup
¾ cup half & half
  1 can (6 ounces) StarKist Solid
     White Tuna, drained and
     chunked
½ pound asparagus, trimmed, cut
     into 1-inch pieces and
     blanched *or* 1 package
     (10 ounces) frozen
     asparagus, thawed and
     drained
½ teaspoon lemon juice
     Freshly ground black pepper to
     taste
¼ cup grated Parmesan cheese
  1 tablespoon minced fresh
     parsley

Cook pasta according to package directions; drain, toss with olive oil. Keep warm. Meanwhile, in medium saucepan, combine soup and half & half; blend well. Stir in tuna, blanched asparagus, lemon juice and black pepper. Heat thoroughly; serve over pasta. Sprinkle with cheese and parsley. *Makes 2 servings*

Prep Time: 15 minutes

Biscuit-Topped Tuna Bake

Savory Rice Pilaf with Tuna

Quick and easy pilaf becomes a main meal with delicious and nutritious tuna.

  2 tablespoons butter or
      margarine
  1 cup long grain white rice
  ½ cup finely chopped onion
  ¼ teaspoon ground black pepper
1½ teaspoons dried basil, crushed
2¼ cups chicken or vegetable
      broth
1½ cups assorted fresh or frozen
      and thawed vegetables*
  1 can (12 ounces) StarKist Solid
      White or Chunk Light Tuna,
      drained and chunked
  ¾ cup shredded Cheddar cheese,
      divided

In medium saucepan with tight-fitting lid, melt butter over medium-high heat; sauté rice and onion until rice is golden and onion is soft. Stir in pepper, basil, chicken broth and vegetables. Bring to a boil; cover. Reduce heat; simmer about 20 minutes or until rice is tender (*not all liquid will be absorbed*). Add tuna and ½ cup cheese, stirring to blend; transfer to serving dish. Sprinkle with remaining ¼ cup cheese.   *Makes 4 servings*

*Suggested vegetables include peas, corn, sliced carrots, broccoli flowerets, sliced zucchini and sliced mushrooms.

Prep Time: 30 minutes

Cheese Ravioli and Albacore

Make this in a jiffy, using refrigerated fresh ravioli and packaged white sauce.

  2 cups Quick White Sauce
      (page 76) *or* 1 envelope
      (1.8 ounces) white sauce,
      prepared
  ½ cup grated Parmesan cheese,
      divided
  ¾ teaspoon garlic salt
  ½ teaspoon ground black pepper
  ½ teaspoon ground nutmeg
  1 cup frozen baby peas, thawed
  1 can (6 ounces) StarKist Solid
      White Tuna, drained and
      chunked
  9 to 10 ounces fresh cheese
      ravioli, prepared according
      to package directions
  1 tablespoon minced fresh
      parsley

In saucepan, combine 2 cups white sauce, ¼ cup cheese and seasonings; heat thoroughly over low heat. Add peas and tuna; heat. Serve over ravioli. Sprinkle with remaining cheese and parsley.
          Makes 6 servings

Note: To make as a casserole, pour ⅓ of sauce in lightly greased 11×7-inch baking dish. Arrange half of cooked ravioli over sauce. Repeat layering ending with sauce. Sprinkle with remaining cheese. Cover; bake in 350°F oven 25 to 30 minutes or until hot. Casserole may be refrigerated overnight before baking; increase baking time to 35 to 45 minutes or until hot.

Prep Time: 30 minutes

Sherried Tuna over Herbed Waffles

This updated version of a family favorite is sure to please. Adding herbs to your favorite waffle batter is a cinch; what a pleasant change from toasted breads!

  2 cups buttermilk biscuit mix
  1 teaspoon herbs de provence
  ¼ teaspoon grated lemon peel
  ¼ teaspoon ground white pepper
  2 cups buttermilk
  1 tablespoon butter or margarine
  1 medium onion, sliced
  1 jar (4½ ounces) sliced mushrooms, drained
  ¼ cup dry sherry
  1 can (10¾ ounces) golden mushroom soup
  ½ cup milk or half & half
  ½ to 1 teaspoon country-style Dijon mustard
  1 can (12 ounces) StarKist Solid White Tuna, drained and chunked

In medium bowl, mix together biscuit mix, herbs de provence, lemon peel and pepper; stir in buttermilk until batter is well blended. Make enough waffles for 6 servings. Place waffles on cooling rack in 325°F oven to keep warm and slightly crisp.

In medium saucepan, melt butter over medium heat; sauté onion until soft. Add mushrooms and sherry; cook over medium-high heat until liquid is reduced by half. Add soup, milk and mustard; blend well. Stir in tuna; heat thoroughly. Serve over crisp herbed waffles.
Makes 6 servings

Prep Time: 20 minutes

Tuna and Rice Skillet Dinner

What could be easier than a one skillet meal?

  1 package (6½ ounces) chicken flavored rice mix
  ½ cup chopped onion
    Water
  1½ cups frozen peas and carrots, thawed
  1 can (10¾ ounces) cream of mushroom soup
  ⅛ teaspoon ground black pepper
  1 can (12 ounces) StarKist Solid White or Chunk Light Tuna, drained and chunked
  ⅓ cup toasted slivered almonds (optional)

In medium saucepan, combine rice mix and onion; add water. Prepare rice according to package directions. Stir in vegetables, soup and pepper; blend well. Simmer, covered, 5 to 7 minutes, stirring occasionally. Stir in tuna; serve with almonds, if desired.
Makes 4 to 6 servings

Prep Time: 30 minutes

Tuna and Pasta Frittata

Frittata, Italian for omelet, has ingredients "scrambled" in with the eggs before cooking and is served flat instead of folded over.

- 1 tablespoon olive oil
- 2 cups cooked spaghetti
- 4 large eggs
- 2 tablespoons milk
- ¼ cup prepared pesto sauce
- 1 can (6 ounces) StarKist Solid White or Chunk Light Tuna, drained and flaked
- ½ cup shredded mozzarella cheese

Preheat broiler. In medium ovenproof skillet, heat oil over medium-high heat; sauté spaghetti. In bowl, combine eggs, milk and pesto sauce; blend well. Add tuna; pour mixture over hot spaghetti. Cook over medium-low heat, stirring occasionally until eggs are almost completely set. Sprinkle cheese over cooked eggs; place under broiler until cheese is bubbly and golden. Serve hot or at room temperature.

Makes 2 to 4 servings

Prep Time: 8 minutes

Tuna with Broccoli and Cheddar

Serve this saucy dish in small French bread loaves.

- 3 cups low fat milk
- 1 envelope (1.8 ounces) white sauce mix
- 2 teaspoons chicken bouillon granules
- 1½ cups shredded Cheddar cheese
- 3 cups cooked chopped broccoli
- ½ teaspoon finely ground black pepper
- ¼ to ½ teaspoon grated lemon peel
- 1 can (12 ounces) StarKist Solid White or Chunk Light Tuna, drained and chunked
- 2 small (8 ounces *each*) round French bread loaves, hollowed out and heated*

In 1½-quart saucepan, combine milk, white sauce mix and bouillon granules, using wire whisk to blend. Cook over medium-high heat, whisking constantly until bouillon dissolves and sauce has thickened slightly. Reduce heat; add cheese, stirring until melted. Stir in broccoli, pepper and lemon peel; heat thoroughly. Add tuna just before serving. Divide mixture between hollowed loaves. Cut into wedges.

Makes 6 servings

*Brush French bread with garlic butter before heating.

Prep Time: 20 minutes

Tuna and Pasta Frittata

Broiled Tomatoes Stuffed with Tuna

Look for Crimini (Italian brown) mushrooms for a special flavor.

- **6 ripe beefsteak tomatoes**
- **1 to 2 tablespoons butter or margarine**
- **1 teaspoon minced or pressed fresh garlic**
- **½ medium onion, cut in half**
- **5 ounces Crimini (Italian brown) mushrooms, cleaned and trimmed***
- **1 can (12 ounces) StarKist Solid White or Chunk Light Tuna, drained and flaked**
- **3 cups French or sourdough coarse fresh breadcrumbs**
- **1 cup shredded mozzarella cheese**
- **Olive oil**

Halve each tomato; use fork to break up cut surface of each half, pressing down to make shallow well. Arrange in baking dish.

In medium skillet, heat butter over low heat; sauté garlic. In food processor bowl with metal blade, finely chop onion; transfer to skillet and sauté until onion is soft. Place mushrooms in food processor bowl; finely mince (*do not over process*).

Transfer mushrooms to skillet; sauté with onion and garlic. In large bowl, combine tuna, sautéed garlic, onion and mushrooms, breadcrumbs and cheese. Fill each tomato with generous ½ cup filling. Drizzle olive oil over filled tomato halves; bake in 450°F oven 10 to 12 minutes until heated through. Place under broiler just until tops are lightly browned and crisp.   *Makes 6 servings*

*Regular domestic white mushrooms may be used.

Tip: To make fresh breadcrumbs, process ½ pound French bread in food processor bowl fitted with metal blade. Freeze remaining breadcrumbs for a later use.

Prep Time: 25 minutes

Potato Tuna au Gratin

A quick and easy family favorite.

- **1 package (5 or 6 ounces) Cheddar cheese au gratin potatoes**
- **1 can (12 ounces) StarKist Solid White or Chunk Light Tuna, drained and chunked**
- **¼ cup chopped onion**
- **1 package (16 ounces) frozen broccoli cuts, cooked and drained**
- **¾ cup shredded Cheddar cheese**
- **¼ cup breadcrumbs**

Prepare potatoes according to package directions. While potatoes are standing, stir in tuna and onion. Arrange cooked broccoli in bottom of lightly greased 11×7-inch baking dish. Pour tuna-potato mixture over broccoli; top with cheese. Broil 3 to 4 minutes or until cheese is bubbly. Sprinkle breadcrumbs over top.
          Makes 6 servings

Prep Time: 35 minutes

Broiled Tomatoes Stuffed with Tuna

Albacore Vegetable Pilaf

Sour cream and lemon bring a fresh and lively taste to this pilaf.

1 cup long grain white rice
1 can (14 1/2 ounces) chicken broth
1/4 cup water
2 to 3 tablespoons lemon juice
1 teaspoon dried dill weed
1/2 teaspoon salt
1/4 teaspoon ground black pepper
1/4 teaspoon garlic powder
1/2 cup chopped red bell pepper
1/2 cup chopped green bell pepper
1/2 cup chopped zucchini
1/2 cup corn
1 cup sour cream
1 can (12 ounces) StarKist Solid White Tuna, drained and chunked

In medium saucepan with tight-fitting lid, combine rice, chicken broth, water, lemon juice, dill, salt, black pepper and garlic powder. Bring to a boil; cover. Reduce heat; simmer 15 minutes. Stir in vegetables; cover and continue cooking 5 to 7 more minutes or until all liquid is absorbed. Stir in sour cream and tuna. Serve hot or cold.   *Makes 6 servings*

Prep Time: 30 minutes

Tuna Cream Cheese Omelets

These omelets make cooking for 1 or 2 a snap.

1 teaspoon butter or margarine
4 to 6 large eggs
   Water
2 ounces cream cheese with chives, cut into 1/2-inch cubes, divided
2 tablespoons drained and chopped roasted red peppers, divided
1 can (6 ounces) StarKist Solid White or Chunk Light Tuna, drained and chunked, divided
1 tablespoon light sour cream, divided
   Salt and pepper to taste

In small nonstick skillet, melt butter over medium-high heat. Beat 2 or 3 large eggs with 1 teaspoon water per egg. Stir in half of cream cheese and half of peppers. Pour into hot skillet; cook, using back of spatula to push cooked portion of eggs toward center, letting liquid flow underneath.

When eggs are cooked on bottom and top is nearly dry, sprinkle half the tuna over half the omelet. Fold omelet in half; slide onto plate. Top with half of sour cream; sprinkle with salt and pepper. Repeat for second omelet.

Makes 2 omelets

Prep Time: 8 minutes

Albacore Vegetable Pilaf

Tuna and Broccoli Fettucini

Enjoy this reduced fat version of creamy fettucini.

4 cups broccoli flowerets
½ pound fettucini noodles
1 cup (8 ounces) part skim
    ricotta cheese
½ cup low fat milk
⅓ cup grated Parmesan cheese
½ teaspoon garlic salt
½ teaspoon Italian herb
    seasoning
    Salt and pepper to taste
1 can (12 ounces) StarKist Solid
    White or Chunk Light Tuna,
    drained and chunked

In large saucepan of boiling water, cook broccoli until crisp-tender. Remove with slotted spoon to serving bowl. In same saucepan, cook fettucini; drain, rinse and add to broccoli. In same saucepan, combine remaining ingredients except tuna; mix well. Heat thoroughly, stirring frequently, until sauce is smooth and thick. Add tuna. Pour over fettucini and broccoli; toss gently.   *Makes 5 servings*

Prep Time: 25 minutes

Tuna Mac and Cheese

Here's the dish that every kid loves; it's ready in a flash.

1 package (7¼ ounces)
    macaroni and cheese dinner
1 can (12 ounces) StarKist Solid
    White or Chunk Light Tuna,
    drained and chunked
1 cup frozen peas
½ cup shredded Cheddar cheese
½ cup milk
1 teaspoon Italian herb
    seasoning
¼ teaspoon garlic powder
    (optional)
1 tablespoon grated Parmesan
    cheese

Prepare macaroni and cheese dinner according to package directions. Add remaining ingredients except Parmesan cheese. Pour into 1½-quart microwavable serving dish. Cover with vented plastic wrap; microwave on HIGH 2 minutes. Stir; continue heating on HIGH 2½ to 3½ more minutes or until cheese is melted and mixture is heated through. Sprinkle with Parmesan cheese.   *Makes 5 to 6 servings*

Prep Time: 20 minutes

Tuna and Broccoli Fettucini

Crunchy Tuna Squares

Roasted red peppers are sold in jars in the supermarket's Italian section.

1 can (12 ounces) StarKist Solid White or Chunk Light Tuna, drained and chunked
1 cup chopped celery
1 cup chopped roasted cashews
½ cup drained sliced water chestnuts
½ cup chopped green onions, including tops
⅓ cup chopped drained roasted red peppers
1½ cups shredded Cheddar cheese, divided
½ cup mayonnaise or light mayonnaise
½ cup sour cream or light sour cream
2 tablespoons lemon juice
¾ teaspoon seasoned salt
1 cup cheese crackers, crushed into coarse crumbs

In medium bowl, place tuna, celery, cashews, water chestnuts, onions, peppers and 1 cup cheese; mix lightly with fork. In small bowl, whisk together mayonnaise, sour cream, lemon juice and seasoned salt. Add to tuna mixture; mix gently.

Spoon into greased 11×7-inch baking pan. Sprinkle with crushed cracker crumbs; top with remaining ½ cup cheese. Bake in 450°F oven 12 to 15 minutes or until mixture bubbles and begins to brown. Let stand several minutes before cutting into 6 squares.

Makes 6 servings

Prep Time: 20 minutes

Tuna Vegetable Medley

These ingredients go together quickly. This recipe is ready from start to finish in 40 minutes.

8 ounces cooked egg noodles
1 package (10 ounces) frozen chopped broccoli, thawed and well drained
1 package (10 ounces) frozen carrots, thawed and well drained
1 cup corn
1 can (10¾ ounces) cream of mushroom soup
1 can (12 ounces) StarKist Solid White or Chunk Light Tuna, drained and chunked
⅔ cup milk
1 cup shredded Swiss, Cheddar or Monterey Jack Cheese
Salt and pepper to taste
¼ cup grated Parmesan cheese

In large bowl, combine all ingredients except Parmesan cheese; mix well. Pour mixture into 2-quart baking dish; top with Parmesan cheese. Bake in 400°F oven 20 to 30 minutes or until thoroughly heated and golden on top.

Makes 6 servings

Prep Time: 40 minutes

Index